Table of Contents

A Rubbing, Scrubbing Snake

"Ewww!" Katie cried. "Look at that snake! What's wrong with it?" Katie and her classmates were visiting the **reptile** house at the zoo. Katie was staring at one of the snakes. It was in an enormous glass box with lots of rocks and plants.

The snake kept scrubbing its head against a rock. Katie thought the snake was just scratching. But suddenly, something strange happened. To Katie, it looked like plastic was peeling from the snake's head.

Tell Me Why

WHY?

Snakes Shed Their Skin

Susan H. Gray

Published in the United States of America by Cherry Lake Publishing
Ann Arbor, Michigan
www.cherrylakepublishing.com

Content Adviser: Andrew M. Durso, PhD candidate at Utah State University and writer of the blog "Life is Short, but Snakes are Long" (http://snakesarelong.blogspot.com/)
Reading Adviser: Marla Conn, ReadAbility Inc

Photo Credits: © Worraket/Shutterstock Images, 5; © Jaymis Loveday/Flickr, 7; © Nathan clifford/ Shutterstock Images, 9; © dabjola/Shutterstock Images, 11; © iWorkAlone/Shutterstock Images, cover, 1, 13; © Joyce Mar/Shutterstock Images, cover, 1, 15; © Matt Jeppson/Shutterstock Images, cover, 1, 17; © TuTheLens/Shutterstock Images, 19; © gorillaimages/Shutterstock Images, 21

Library of Congress Cataloging-in-Publication Data

Gray, Susan Heinrichs, author.
  Snakes shed their skin / Susan H. Gray.
    pages cm.—(Tell me why . . .)
  Summary: "Young children are naturally curious about animals. Snakes Shed Their Skin offers answers to their most compelling questions about why snakes shed periodically. Age-appropriate explanations and appealing photos encourage readers to continue their quest for knowledge. Additional text features and search tools, including a glossary and an index, help students locate information and learn new words."—Provided by publisher.
  Audience: Ages 6–10
  Audience: K to grade 3
  Includes bibliographical references and index.
  ISBN 978-1-63362-616-4 (hardcover)—ISBN 978-1-63362-706-2 (pbk.)—ISBN 978-1-63362-796-3 (pdf)—ISBN 978-1-63362-886-1 (ebook) 1. Snakes—Behavior—Juvenile literature. 2. Molting—Juvenile literature. 3. Children's questions and answers. [1. Snakes.] I. Title. II. Series: Tell me why (Cherry Lake Publishing)

QL666.O6G682 2016
597.96—dc23

2014048650

Cherry Lake Publishing would like to acknowledge the work of the Partnership for 21st Century Skills. Please visit www.p21.org for more information.

Printed in the United States of America
Corporate Graphics

Zoos often have snake exhibits.

A zoo worker came over to Katie. "The snake is just fine," she said. "It's shedding its skin. Snakes do this from time to time."

Katie kept watching. The snake would rest a little while. Then it would scrub against something. Rest and scrub, rest and scrub.

The zoo worker called the whole class over. "Today, our snake is doing something interesting. Let me tell you about it."

Visit a zoo or park that has reptile displays. Ask if any other reptiles shed their skins.

When a snake sheds, it starts from its head.

Bye-Bye, Skin!

The zoo worker began to explain. "The snake is peeling off a layer of skin. This is called **molting**. Scientists also call it **ecdysis**. Only the outermost layer of skin comes off."

Katie kept watching. The zoo worker continued, "Before molting, the skin gets loose. Then molting begins. It always starts at the head. The snake rubs its face against something rough. Then the skin begins to split."

All snakes shed, including pythons like this one.

The zoo worker said the skin peels back when the snake moves forward. "Usually the skin comes off in one big piece," she said. "Molting usually takes about half an hour. After molting, the snake's color is brighter. Its eyes become clear again, too."

Katie was amazed at everything she heard. But she wanted to know more. She wondered *why* snakes molt. Maybe she could learn more at her school's library.

LOOK!

Shed skins like this one are always wrong-side out. Why do you think this is?

Snakeskins are often left wherever the snake was when it shed.

A Life of Shedding

Katie began to read. Soon she found the answer to her question. She learned that snakes keep growing their whole lives. But the outer layer of skin does not grow. For a snake to get bigger, the old skin has to come off. This is why snakes shed.

As babies, snakes grow very quickly. They shed quite often. But as they get older, growth slows down. Adults might shed only two or three times a year.

These young snakes are growing quickly and will shed many times before they become adults.

A few days before it molts, the snake produces fluid beneath its old skin. The fluid helps the skin to peel off. A healthy snake sheds its skin in one piece. If a snake is sick, its skin comes off in pieces. If its **environment** is too dry, it pulls off in shreds. A snake with skin problems will not shed properly, either.

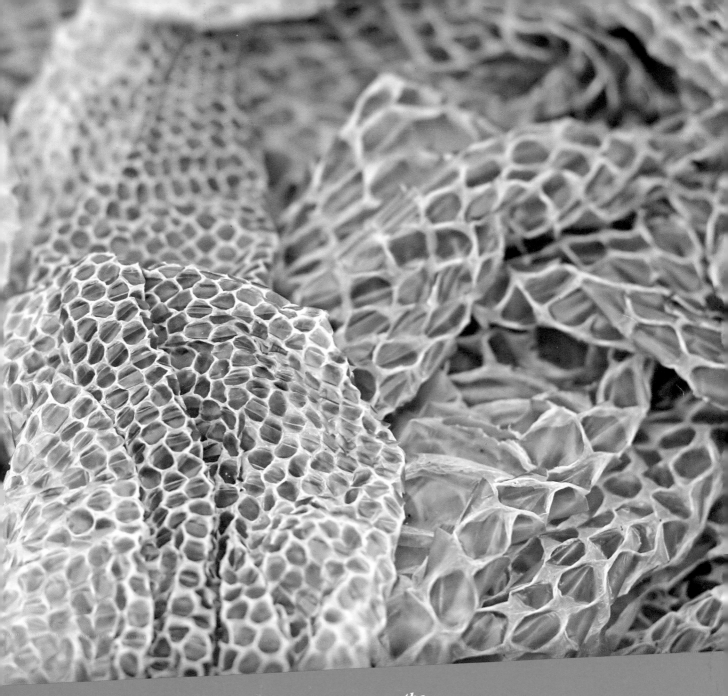

Skin that has been shed has the same pattern as the snake's body, but it is colorless.

Snakes do not have eyelids. Instead, the eyes are covered by special scales. These are clear scales that form caps over the eyes. Before a molt, fluid fills the eye caps. The fluid makes the eyes look cloudy and makes it difficult for the snake to see. The snake is a bit helpless at this time. It may hide out until molting is over.

MAKE A GUESS!

Snake owners often watch for their snakes to molt. Then they spray water into their cages. Why would they do that?

You can tell this eastern garter snake is going to start shedding soon because its eyes are blue and cloudy.

Yummy, Yummy Skin

Snakes are not alone in shedding their skins. Frogs and lizards also shed. Often, frogs will twist and squirm around first. This helps to loosen up the skin. After they shed, they eat the old skin. This way, they recycle **nutrients** back into their bodies.

Insects and spiders also molt. A **cicada** splits its shell down the back. The insect climbs out, leaving its old skin behind.

Humans also shed their skin. Usually, the pieces are so small that you don't notice. But your skin may come off in bigger pieces after you've been sunburned.

This Argentine red tegu, a type of lizard, is molting.

Many zoos have great snake displays. State and national parks often keep snakes, too. Some zoo workers and park rangers are snake experts. They know which snake **species** live in the area. They can tell you what the snakes eat. They might even have shed skins that you can touch and hold. Now that you understand why snakes shed their skin, you might not say "Ewww!" if you see it happen!

If a snake isn't dangerous, a snake handler might let you touch it. This is an albino burmese python.

Think About It!

The snake seems nervous before and during a molt. It becomes more ready to strike. Snake owners try not to handle their pets at this time. Why do you think snakes act this way?

Like snakes, lizards also shed their skin. But unlike snakes, most lizards have eyelids. Some lizards prepare for ecdysis by doing a strange thing. They puff their eyes way out. Why would they do such a thing?

Shedding always starts at the snake's head. But what if it began at the tip of the tail? Would that cause problems for the snake? If so, what problems might arise?

Glossary

cicada (sih-KEY-duh) a large type of flying insect

ecdysis (EK-duh-sis) the act of shedding an outer coat or skin

environment (en-VYE-ruhn-muhnt) the natural surroundings of living things, such as the air, land, and sea

molting (MOLT-eeng) losing old fur, feathers, a shell, or skin so that new ones can grow

nutrients (NOO-tree-uhnts) substances that living things need to grow and stay healthy

reptile (REP-tile) a cold-blooded animal with a backbone and scales that breathes air and reproduces on land; most reptiles have four legs and reproduce by laying eggs

species (SPEE-sheez) one type, or kind, of plant or animal

Find Out More

Books:

Gibbons, Gail. *Snakes.* New York: Holiday House, 2010.

O'Neill, Amanda. *I Wonder Why Snakes Shed Their Skin and Other Questions About Reptiles.* New York: Kingfisher, 2011.

Stewart, Melissa. *Snakes!* Washington, DC: National Geographic Society, 2009.

Web Sites:

Enchanted Learning: Snake Printouts
www.enchantedlearning.com/subjects/reptiles/snakes/printouts.shtml
Take a quiz about snakes, make a snake craft, or print out coloring pages.

Kids' Inquiry of Diverse Species: Common Snakes
www.biokids.umich.edu/critters/Colubridae/
This page has links to information about many different species of snakes.

Life is Short, but Snakes are Long: Identifying snake sheds, part III
http://snakesarelong.blogspot.com/2012/11/identifying-snake-sheds-part-iii.html
Did you find some snakeskin? With some help from an adult, use this article to try to identify the species of snake that shed it.

Index

About the Author

Susan H. Gray has a master's degree in zoology. She has worked in research and has taught college-level science classes. Susan has also written more than 140 science and reference books, but especially likes to write about animals. She and her husband, Michael, live in Cabot, Arkansas.